Amazon Fba for Beginners

The Ultimate Guide to Generate a Passive Income by Taking Advantage of Amazon Platform

Donald White

TABLE OF CONTENTS

#shipyard
Thursday, February 28th
MacBook Pro

INTRODUCTION

If you're reading this book, you've probably heard of Amazon FBA and the opportunity, as some say, to make good money with it.

In fact, in this book we will not only analyze what Amazon FBA is and how it works, but we will suggest some small tips on how to optimize your sales. With that knowledge, a little field practice and a bit of business acumen, Amazon FBA can become not only a source of income, but also a great way to get rich.

But is all that glitters really gold? Can you really make money with amazon FBA? Or has competition reached a level in 2020 that it no longer has the possibility of entering an already saturated market, especially on the international scene?

The purpose of this book is to answer all these questions and shed light on this business opportunity, so loved but also criticized by those who make money differently.

Enjoy the reading!!

Chapter 1 e-bay Vs. Amazon

Usually, there is no competition between the two platforms. The real thing is dependent on you and what you really want. This might sound somehow strange, so let's take a knife to it and break it down.

eBay

Over the years, eBay is like one mighty flea market, the sellers are doing most if not all of the jobs, like setting up your 'stand.' You will handle transactions, offer product, ship it, and perform all the things involved to make sales and purchase a complete chain. You have a 100% responsibility here.

The reason why this chapter begins with 'it's up to you' is that though it seems like a lot of work, there are benefits in it. One of the advantages is that you will earn more when you are doing more of the work. A larger percentage of the profit will be completely yours, or you will be having more of it than in a situation where someone else or a team is handling it for you.

Amazon FBA

We aren't looking at Amazon as a whole but Amazon FBA specifically. So how does that look like in the setting we are talking about?

This is like one big mall where you own a shop. There are storekeepers who work for everyone and help them sell their items. Once you sign up for the program, you will get a space in the warehouse. You will pay for it of course, but it also means that when you are at home sleeping or watching your favorite show, some is handling shipping, packing and

delivering your items to your buyer's location.

Of course, the benefit is more than that, and we have

explained most of it. The most important one we shouldtalk about here are the charges you will pay for using the services.

Well, you can sell on both channels using Amazon.

You haven't forgotten Multi-Channel Fulfillment, have you? You will keep your item with Amazon, and they will do the job of shipping and delivering the item when people make an order on Amazon or on the other platforms.

Go to your seller account. Choose to create Multi-Channel Shipment to a channel like eBay. Let Amazon fill the submitted orders. They will also manage the orders you have submitted. Things will even be easier if you are using a professional account. Amazon can automatically fulfill the FBA inventory with MCF.

Chapter 2 How to Use Seller Central To Upload Inventory, Create Shipping Plan, Get Paid, and...

Using Amazon Seller Central is not that complicated as it seems to be. Let us see how you can use it.

Using Seller Central to get Payments
For initiating transmission of funds to your bank account from your seller account, Amazon Payments needs:

- Valid information of your credit card for billing and verification purposes.
- Valid information concerning your bank account to which you want the funds to be transferred.

After a sale takes place, and you confirm with Amazon that you have shipped the order, Amazon starts the process of payment from the account of buyer. However, in the case that it is an Amazon FBA order, Amazon will credit your account once they shipped out the order. The net proceeds of the sale are credited to your account. It is also important to note that the refunds to customers and selling fees are debited against the funds credited to your account.

The payments in your seller account are credited every 14 days. Amazon transfers the funds once Amazon Payments deduces that your funds do not need to be held to cover the charges, A-to-Z guarantee claims, refunds or other declarations against your transactions of sales. For receiving payments, you must mention the details of a US checking account/ UK bank account/ Eurozone bank account (Austria, Cyprus, Estonia, Belgium, Finland, France, Greece, Ireland, Germany, Italy, Luxembourg, the Netherlands,

Malta, Portugal, Slovenia, Slovakia, and Spain)/ New Zealand,

Australia, India, Canada or Hong Kong.

When you need to ship your orders yourself
Amazon handles all the packaging, labelling and shipping on its own for your Amazon FBA products. But if you are working under the process of Amazon Merchant Shipping, you have to handle the shipping yourself.

Shipping, managing and selling your products
You can put buttons and allow clicks on your websites to sell your merchandize. You can check your requests and orders daily with the help of "Manage Orders" in Seller Central. You must ship the orders as soon as possible to gain customer loyalty.

Confirm the shipments
You need to confirm your shipment with Amazon and tell them the details of date of sending, the carrier used and other tracking information regarding the package. If you confirm the shipment, Amazon charges the customers. And, if you do not verify the shipment, your payment will not be initiated. The order is cancelled if you do not initiate the shipment after 30 days of order. You must sign in to Seller Central often. A notice will be displayed on the home page if any of your orders are in danger of cancellation.

Inventory Loader
If you want to upload multiple listings in one file to match against existing pages of products, you have to use Inventory Loader at Amazon.com. You cannot use it to create new pages of products. You can add new stock, amend existing items, and delete or "zero" your stock for items that are not available. You can also cleanse and replace all your listings with one upload only.

Since you are only modifying your stock, you do not have to provide product data in complete detail as you would when you use a category specific file of inventory. You can also use Inventory Loader to upload and modify your listings in multiple categories of products at the same time.

Using Seller Central to create Shipping Creation

Workflow

You can create your shipment to the fulfillment centers of Amazon with the following steps of shipping creation workflow:

- Place Quantity
- Put Products In order
- Label Products
- Preview Consignment
- Prepare Consignment
- Summary

First of all, you need to choose your products in the inventory you want to ship to the company. You can do it using the "Manage FBA Inventory" or "Manage Inventory" page ofthe Seller Central. Select the product you want to transport, choose Send/ Replenish Inventory from the drop down menu of "Apply to Selected Items(s)" on Manage FBA Inventory page. The next page of Send/ Replenish Inventory will require you to take the following decisions:

Make a shipping plan/ Add to an Open Shipping Plan: In case you have an existing shipping plan, you can choose the plan from the drop down plan after you select "Add to an Existing Shipping Plan".

Verify your ship-from address: The address you had entered can be used to ship your consignment. If you wish to edit it, you can enter a fresh ship-from address.

Select the type of packing: You need to select case-packed products or individual products.

After you are done with all these steps, select "Continue to shipping plan" tab to start your workflow.

Send your FBA Inventory to Amazon

After you are set to send your inventory to Amazon, the next step is to create a shipping plan. It is a list of items which you wish to send to the fulfillment centers of Amazon. Your seller account has a shipment creation tool, which makes it simpler to select the items you wish to send, your shipment method, the quantity of the products, whether you wish to label the products yourself or Amazon should do it. You can also procure printable shipping and product labels from the shipping creation tools along with the guidance to prepare your items for shipment.

Once you are ready with your shipment plan, you can start preparing and packing your items in order to ship them to the Amazon fulfillment centers. You can break your shipping plan into various multiple shipments, which are directed to different Amazon fulfillment centers. This brings your products closer to your customers in different regions.

Chapter 3 How to Create Bundle To Eliminate Competition

You cannot ignore the competition on Amazon even if you want to. There are many fast selling products on Amazon which can overtake your products if you become lazy and do not take the competition seriously. People often become tired of competing with the swarm of sellers on your product page of Amazon. You need to look for different ways to raise your margins and trade more products. If you aspire that you had something exclusive to offer on the website, you need to take one step ahead. You do not need to private label or import your products to stand ahead of the crowd. You just need to create your own Amazon bundles. You must be wondering what are Amazon bundles.

Amazon bundles are exclusive products which you build yourself by joining two or more compatible, existing products into one bundle. Retail arbitrage products can be bundled together. Wholesale products can be bundled together. Imported products can also be bundled. Moreover, you can also bundle together all the three kinds of products.

Bundling the products together is a very effective method to stay ahead, at least three steps, of the competition. You do not need to have a very high budget for creating bundles.

Use your present method of sourcing to create bundles

You can sell your bundle and earn higher margin since you have an exclusive product in demand. Sometimes, several units are sold in just one day. You can own the product page of Amazon and the Buy Box as well. This keeps you ahead of competition. You can also create high demand by creating bundles of seasonal products. Moreover, you do not have to look for new providers of products if you repurpose saturated inventory. All your products can be sold in all categories of Amazon even if you offer entry level bundlesor premium bundles.

The hurdles with bundles

Creating bundles does sound great but it is not so simple. Every bundle is not created equally. Not any random products can be bundled and sold like that. They will not sell for sure. You need to know what products you should bundle together to make maximum profits.

Important things to note while creating bundles You must create bundles of products which are in demand. Create the product page of Amazon correctly so that buyers can easily find it in their search. It is equally important to price the bundles correctly to hit on target. Overpriced bundles will not sell. Choose the correct goods to bundle together. If you do not know how to bundle goods, you must go through the guidelines of bundling by Amazon. Otherwise, your listings may be cancelled. Another most important thing is to pass your bundle through the test of profitability factor.

A perfect bundle is the one which gives maximum value to the customers and the products are complimentary to each other. You must read the *Amazon's Product Bundling Policy in Seller Central* before you proceed to create your own bundles. You will also need to buy your own UPC (Universal Product Code) to list your bundle on Amazon.

When a bundle cannot be called a bundle?

A multi-pack cannot be categorized as a bundle. For example, you cannot call eight pairs of white socks as a bundle. If a bundle is just a variation of the parent product, you cannot call it a bundle.

When you do not need to buy a UPC

If your products fall into the following categories, you do not require buying a new UPC. The UPC on the product itself can be used.

Home & Garden Kitchen & Dining

Bedding & Bath Furniture & Décor Appliances

Arts, Sewing & Crafts Lawn, Patio & Garden Home Improvement

Pet Supplies

Lamps & Light Fixtures Hand & Power Tools Bath & Kitchen

Fixtures Building Supplies Hardware

Grocery & Gourmet Foods Sports & Outdoors Outdoor Recreation

Fitness & Exercise

Cycling

Fishing & Hunting Boating & Water Sports

Outdoor & Athletic Clothing Team Sports

Sports Collectibles Fan Shop

Golf

All Outdoors & Sports

If your products fall beyond these categories mentioned above, you would require buying a new UPC in favor of your multipack.

amazon

Chapter 4 Understanding Amazon's Success

Chances are you're fairly familiar with Amazon from the perspective of a buyer. They sell goods from a multitude of companies, including individuals who list their own items, and offer everything from digital products like music and e- books to physical products like home goods, toys, video games, and almost anything you can possibly think of ordering.

As the name might suggest, Amazon is huge much like the body of water that it's named after. Every single month they average more than 65 million buyers. That's 65 million customers all spending money through one interface, on one website, every single month. A large part of their success has been marketing and fulfilling those marketing promises, such as secure shopping, comparably low prices, and perks like free shipping for orders that qualify. In addition, Amazon has such a large array of items that it can almost virtually replace the need to ever leave the home to shop.

The largest reason Amazon is successful is because they are customer-centric. They cater to the buyer. As businessmen have always said, "The customer is always right." Amazon has lived by this motto while still going out of their way to improve the seller's experience as well.

Why You Should Use Amazon as a Seller

While being a buyer-oriented online shopping experience means that the buyer is almost always going to be able to get the upper-hand in disputes and other exchanges, it is still of the utmost importance to realize that Amazon is often the best possible place to sell your goods online. This is true for a couple reasons.

Firstly, Amazon has locked down the concept of the all-encompassing online shopping portal, and taking advantage of its many ways to produce an income is well documented and relatively easy compared to creating an online store or other online service from scratch. Their one-stop shopping experience provides more than you can provide on your own website, and unless you're ready to invest millions of dollars and years of hard work, it's unlikely that you'll be able to effectively compete with them on your own.

Secondly, the costs of getting started are minimal when compared to setting up your own online sales channels. While it may be tempting to try to avoid Amazon's fees, the truth is that a higher sales volume on Amazon and the initial cost of startup and maintaining a seller presence is much more expensive than these fees will typically be. Even if you are going to start an online store yourself, not having an Amazon presence means lost opportunities to reach the largest number of buyers in the world. Since the costs are lower to start with Amazon, it's obviously the best choice to start here and work on expanding later if that is your goal.

New and Used

One great advantage of Amazon, for both buyers and sellers, is that they not only list items that are brand new, but they also list items that are in various conditions. Having the option to sell used (and sometimes even rare) itemsthrough a safe and secure platform like Amazon means that nearly anything can be sold or bought through the same platform. While the ability to price the items you sell (and see everyone else's pricing) means more competition, this isn't as huge of a concern as one might think. We'll talk about that more later.

Customer Involvement

Another great thing about Amazon is that with a large amount of customers comes a huge amount of people that are interacting with the website past the point of purchase. This extends past simply writing reviews, but these reviews are of the utmost importance.

Traditionally, a person would go into a store, look at a product, possibly get to handle it for a few moments, and then have to decide if the price tag fit their expectations and limited knowledge of the item. This not only takes a lot of time, but the results are lackluster at best. There are very few ways to decide if a $1,000 laptop is worth $500 more than the $500 laptop sitting directly next to it. This is especially true if their technical specs are relatively similar. The internet has improved this through the use of customer reviewers. When it comes to customer reviews, Amazon tends to have the most reviews available per product when compared to other sites. This is true because they have a huge customer base, but it is also true because Amazon actively encourages members to take the time to let others know if they were happy with a product or not.

This translates into more sales for products that review well with purchasers. Where a dedicated website for selling products may be able to provide a really well written review from the content creators, the huge amount of customers willing to post reviews on Amazon can sometimes lead to HUNDREDS of opinions on a product. Similarly, when a product is bought a lot, it is hoisted to the top of the best seller lists that Amazon generates based on automated algorithms. As a seller, this means that if you are looking to pick up products that are highly desirable, it is easy for you to determine what products (or at least what type of products) are being sold regularly. This customer involvement and automated calculations done by Amazon allows you some detailed insight into the market(s) you are most likely to venture into.

Next, let's discuss the difference between selling on Amazon and selling on Amazon using their Fulfillment by Amazon services.

Chapter 5 Quality Control

Quality control is something that you should always have in mind.

Confirming the product at your first order is only one little part when talking about quality control. In fact, you should be thinking about quality control already when searching for suppliers.

I already mentioned earlier that once you are searching for suppliers on Alibaba, you should always find out where do they supply the most and you can always ask. However, even before reaching out to them on Alibaba there is a click of a button that will give you a nice overview of the factory's main transaction history.

With this example I can already assume that it might not be a good idea to use this supplier if you want to sell the product in Japan or Germany.

Of course you might take the advantage of being the first who does it. However, the standards and people's requirements differ in many countries.

I am relating this example to quality control already as some products are considered to be a good quality in the US, but might be very low for the UK, or vice versa.

As for a supplier who provides low prices, and thinking that will make it on the US market, you should make sure that the main transaction history for the same supplier is indeed the US market.

Next, you should be ordering samples as I explained before by comparing multiple suppliers' product as well as making sure they are using safe packaging for delivery.

Once you have chosen the right supplier and already private labeled your sample product, you must be very vigilant and try to find as many mistakes as possible, faults, or defects right at the beginning.

In case there is a problem or fault with the OEM sample order and you assume that in higher volume those defects will disappear, then you really should think again.

Any careless attitude you display will reflect on your product, and your suppliers will never spend more money on your product, neither will they work harder unless you make them do so.

That being said, you must always exhibit an attitude towards your product like a real business, and always look at the quality, and if there is any direction you want to go it is only to create better and better quality, and your suppliers must be on the same page.

In order to make sure that your suppliers are always on the same page with you, everything must be documented, not only to remind them about your expectations, but to make sure they understand who dictates the terms in regards to the quality.

I do understand that there are some awesome employees out there who never required being baby sited; how-ever you can only be 100% sure if you really do everything in your power to keep it that way.

I don't mean to be iron feast, and you must appreciate the hard work they do for you, and should mention often that you are very happy with the factory. And when your business is going very well, you should show your face by visiting the factory workers. You can also take the factory manager out for a dinner, if you can afford it at least once a year.

Back to documentation, as that's one of the key things that you must practice at all times.

At first if you really want to make sure that everything goes well, you must have a plan for your first large order in regards to quality check. There are many suppliers that when they send out one or two samples they will make sure that it is very well presented. However, once you move on a high volume production you can experience faulty products, and it's vital to have a written plan in order to avoid conflicts that could happen.

There are multiple ways to achieve this; some might cost you lots, like hiring a third party inspection company. However, you might ask your suppliers to carry out self-inspections before shipping.

There is an excellent technique that I used at first, and even since then, and it's completely free. What you do is that you ask your supplier to provide pictures at each phase of the production.

1st Picture:
Once the product comes off the production line and still with no logo on it; It must be the right measurements as well as colours.

2nd Picture:
Once the product has been created, and your logo is visible on it. You might also order an English user guide that also has your logo on it, which you might also want to see and confirm before shipping.

3rd Picture:
The product already in your OEM packaging.

4th Picture:
Once all products are in the box that will be shipped, while the box is still open

5th Picture:
Photo of the Box/Boxes that are now ready to be shipped, clearly visible with the shipping label.

All the above mentioned must be confirmed before placing the order and must be written on the Sales Agreement / Purchasing Agreement.

The reason is that you have to understand that mistakes can be made by your supplier, and it's your responsibility to spot them as early as possible in order to minimize your cost.

An example here is you spot a fault when it comes off the production line, when there is no logo on the product, it will cost lot less to the factory to improve it. However, once they do the screen printing on all 100, or more units, that will be more cost to them and more delay to you.

Stage 2, once there is logo on the product, and you might spot that the logo is not positioned the way you want, or they have used the wrong colour, you must tell them that right then. And you should proceed the same way in regards to the packaging, as well as with the user guide in case you will have that.

Let's say that your products are already shipped to you, and you receive it with all above mentioned faults, you might choose to send it back, but that will cost you so much, and probably your suppliers will not take it back anyways... Or try to sell it that way at a cheaper price, hoping someone will buy the faulty products, or you might as well just bin them.

The worse that can happen is that you didn't spot any of the faults but customers receiving the products did. This can be very bad for your reputation and you will have difficulties creating a good name for your brand.

I hope all that makes sense. Also realize there are plenty of tasks to do, but believe me all this little steps matter in order to be successful, especially if you want to sell your products on Amazon.

MacBook Pro

Chapter 6 Is Amazon FBA the Right Service for Me?

If you have a passion for buying and selling, the yes, Amazon FBA is the ideal business platform to consider. After all, since you already love online retail anyway, why not take it a step further and try to make some money out of it? With FBA, what you are doing is scouring for items (shopping) and then reselling them to other customers. Amazon has already made the job easier for you by taking away the worry about storage space, sales, shipping and customer support. All you needto do is find the products you are passionate about selling and get started.

Here is how you can tell whether Amazon FBA is the perfect online business and passive income stream for you:

- You are looking for a long-term side hustle that is dependable.
- You are looking for extra income aside from your regular 9-5 job.
- You want an additional way of making money online, but from the comfort of your home.
- You have always wanted to dabble in entrepreneurship without taking too much risk that is going to land you in debt.

In addition, Amazon FBA is not going to be the perfect business model for you if:

- You are hoping this is going to be a shortcut to getting rich quickly (no such shortcut like that exists, unfortunately).

- You are hoping to make massive profits in a short amount of time.

- You are looking for a quick return on the investment that you put in.

- You do not have the time to commit to doing the necessary work.

Quick Stats and Facts about Amazon's FBA Service

For those who are new to the Amazon FBA scene, here are some quick and important facts that you should keep abreast of. One, more than one Amazon marketplace exists and it depends on where your customers are located. A customer's location is going to determine which Amazon.com store they see. The location will also determine which fulfillment service your customers experience.

Picture 2

By far, Amazon's largest marketplace is none other than the United States of course, which also happens to be the most active marketplace compared to the rest. Amazon's marketplaces are divided into the following categories:

In North America, the marketplaces are:

- *Canada*
- *Mexico*

- United States

In Europe:

- *Spain*
- *Germany*

- United Kingdom
- *France*
- *Italy*

In Asia:

- *India*
- *China*
- *Japan*

Each marketplace's website address will reflect its location. Amazon in the UK, for example, is accessed via Amazon.co.uk. In France, the address would be Amazon.fr, in Japan it's Amazon.co.jp and so on. The location of each marketplace would determine the specific regulations and tax laws, which apply locally depending on the country and region, which you would need to familiarize yourself with before you set up your FBA business.

By default, for most sellers based in the U.S., the marketplace would, of course, be Amazon.com. However, sellers do have the option of branching out and diversifying their products into other regions if they wanted to. The advantage of doing that is you are expanding your services and potentially boosting revenue, but the downside is you might have to deal with higher costs when it comes to shipping. You will also need to have the time to commit to managing different stores in different regions. If you cannot, you will need to have the necessary funds to hire help in managing and operating your multiple stores.

Now, if you are happy just with running a simple retail store with no plans for expansion, then you will not need an e- Commerce website to sell on FBA. However, if you want to take your business a step further, then an e-Commerce store is the way to do. That decision would depend entirely on what your business goals are. One advantage of having an e- Commerce store operating outside Amazon is the opportunity to increase the visibility of your business and products, which means you are increasing your chances of selling more.

Several other reasons to consider an e-Commerce store include:

- More options to explore selling your products other than what is offered by Amazon.
- You get to implement various other strategies to scale your business.
- Opportunity to build on brand equity.
- Opportunity to increase your market reach through advertising.
- Opportunity to build a solid customer base.
    - Opportunity to build an email list.
    - Opportunity to generate B2B sales
    - Better flexibility with products if it is your own

website.

Benefits of Using Amazon as a Selling Platform

For an online business to be deemed a success, it needs to be efficient and fast when it comes to shipping (among other things). Amazon has already perfected this aspect into an unbeatable process, going the extra mile to ensure that their shipping is always top-notch. They have been doing this ever since Amazon first went live and they have only improved on their shipping service over time. A large part of why customers keep coming back to Amazon is because of their renowned ability to get their orders to customers in the fastest time possible, no matter where in the world the customer may be.

Among the primary reasons sellers want to do business on Amazon's platform is because when you sell on Amazon, you automatically open up to a huge customer base with a high conversion rate. This is something you are not going to be able to replicate on any other e-commerce platform, eBay included. You are able to make more money by doing less work than you normally would on other platforms. Amazon also offers significant advantages, especially for sellers seeking to reach a large and diverse clientele that is ready to spend money online, in a short amount of time.

Amazon has - and always will - put their customers first above anything. The company continues to strive to create better shopping experiences; even going so far as to try to improve their shipping times so they can deliver products even faster than what they are already doing. It also continues to work hard to improve the overall shopping experience customers get when they come to their website. When you sell on Amazon, you are selling with the best of the best. The other benefits you stand to gain include:

- *A Willing and Ready Customer Base* - Amazon's power lies in its large customer base, all of whom are ready and willing to purchase products that they need. By selling on Amazon, compared to many other retail platforms, the number of potential customers is more than triple the number of potential customers on eBay. This means you have an incredible opportunity in your hands. The chance to reach an ever-ready crowd, ready to buy online the minute they set up their business using Amazon. Sellers on Amazon can reach 237 million customers.

- *Customer Spending Power* - Customers love retail shopping. More importantly, they love retail shopping on Amazon more than any other platform. Amazon's revenue in June 2018 surged to $81.76 billion. Consequently, eBay reported $17.05 billion in that same period. An RBC survey even revealed that the average customer who shops on Amazon would spend approximately $320 annually. These numbers are very promising from a seller's point of view. It is an opportunity for sellers to gain depth and breadth where the visibility of their business is concerned.

    - *Its Undisputed Reputation* - Amazon has a credible reputation. When it comes to credibility, no other platform can hold a candle to Amazon, thanks to its exceptional customer service and shipping. This has enabled Amazon to hold a large market share of online consumers simply because of their amazing services. This is something to keep in mind if you are deciding between eBay and Amazon.

    -

- *The Power of Prime* - Amazon Prime can absolutely increase your revenues and increase the number of customers. With Prime, Amazon encourages customers to spend a little bit more by giving incentives such as two- day free shipping on plenty of Prime products. Prime customers spent an average of $528 a year compared to $320 spent by non-Prime Amazon customers.

- *Absence of Listing Fees* - While some platforms charge fees just to list products, Amazon does not. You will only be charged when you have made a sale. As a seller, this means you can list as many items as you would like on Amazon and then leave them until a customer has purchased them. The slight downside with this one is, the sales fee is rather hefty, with Amazon taking at least 20% of the profit. This fee is even higher if you are an FBA seller but of course, when you become an FBA seller, you are doing less work, therefore it balances out in the end.

- *No Relisting Needed* - A huge, hassle-free advantage that Amazon has over platforms like eBay is there is no need to continuously relist your items the way you would need to on eBay. Unless you sign up for the FBA service though, you are going to have to handle the shipping and customer service aspect of the business yourself.

- *You Can Charge Slightly Higher Prices* - Customers would be willing to pay the extra too, for the sake of the guarantee that comes with Amazon. Amazon, at the end of the day, is an online retailer. Like other retailers, they make their money by selling items at competitive rates. This process contrasts with that of a wholesaler, who charges you the lowest possible price, especially if you buy in bulk. eBay acts as a wholesale market and charges the lowest price. For example, a t-shirt may cost $15 on eBay but on Amazon, the same t-shirt might cost you $20. The reason for this increase is that Amazon sells new items (although there are used options available for certain products too), whereas eBay sells mostly used items.

- *Home of Reliable Brands* - Amazon stocks some ofthe most reliable brands on the market. As one of the most trusted retail names out there, Amazon and many of its customers are willing to pay $99 a year to be part of the Prime service. If you sell your products through Amazon, your business is then associated with a trusted brand. If you are a budding brand or the average online entrepreneur trying to make ends meet, Amazon is a good starting point. You get to access their large customerbase while you learn the ropes of the business, before expanding to sell your products on shelves like Walmart.

- *An Excellent Learning Platform* - Business is a risk, but you can minimize that risk when you sell on Amazon. You can use the Amazon platform to test your target market for the products you plan to sell. By selling on Amazon, you gain access to retail data that enables youto see how your product is doing, what the demand is and what you can charge for your product.

- *Driving Awareness* - Amazon can be a great tool used to drive traffic to your other websites. Even better if you have a social media account or blog. It can be a valuable source of buyer information, which can give you great input on how to sell your products from what offers customers like, what they do not like, best times to open for promotions and so on. This should be part of your marketing strategy, to plan for long-term and sustainable success.

- *Perks of Amazon Associates* - You can take advantage of Amazon Associates services to market and promote products related to the industry on your website. Amazon Associates is an affiliate program that allows sellers to earn commissions through affiliate links. A slight downside with this option here is that there will be a clash of interest on the products you sell and the ones you promote. One way to avoid this conflict is by selecting products you promote meticulously and not burn your business.

- *Getting A Boost in Sales of 30-50%* - This boost primarily comes from Amazon's Prime program. Many shoppers do not like the idea of having to pay for shipping and Prime and stepped up to solve that problem. As a Prime user, you are entitled to 2-days of free shipping on any Prime-eligible products. This, in turn, increases the shopper's probability of purchases. Combine that with the "trust factor", where Amazon has built an undisputed reputation for itself and your sales are going to jump exponentially. When a customer sees the "Shipped by Amazon" or "Fulfilled by Amazon" indicator, there is a sense of relief and peace of mind. They know their products are safe and they are not going to be scammed, which is a very real probability if they were to purchase from an unknown merchant with no long-standing history.

- *You do not have to worry about Shipping* - You would be surprised at how tedious and time consuming the shipping and handling process can be. Once again, it is a huge relief for merchants, knowing that Amazon is going to take care of all of that for them. Amazon is the expert when it comes to shipping and they have gone to great lengths to ensure continued quality service, in the fastest and most reliable way. This gives FBA sellers a wonderful and must-not-miss opportunity to capitalize on that. Sellers get to save a lot of time and resources, which they would otherwise have to divert towards handling the shipping aspect. With that out of the way, you are left free and clear to focus entirely on advertising and marketing your products.

- *You Gain the Trust of Your Customers* - With products guaranteed to arrive, customers will love any business running under Amazon and its FBA label. It is not only Americans that love and trust Amazon either. Customers around the world have been turning to the retail giant for years to have their needs met. It is irrefutable what those three simple words "*Fulfilled by Amazon*" can do for your sales figures. Even if the customer has never heard of you until you, they will be completely comfortable purchasing from you, thanks again to the level of trust that is associated with Amazon. Shoppers are more likely to purchase from a retailer they know without a doubt that they can trust.

- *You are Automatically Eligible for Prime* - With 64% of American households being members of Amazon Prime that is almost 85 million customers who are currently using this premier service. Those who are members of Prime are *not* going to buy products that are not eligible for the Prime option. Having that Prime logo is tapping into the trust factor once again and when it comes to selling on Amazon FBA, Prime is definitely the way to go.

- *You Get Access to the "Buy Box"* - Amazon's "buy box" is the white box, which is located on the right, the same section where customers can click on the "Add to Cart" or "Buy Now" options. If you are wondering why this box matters so much, here is why. On Amazon, you will find two types of sellers. One is Amazon themselves; the second is third party. The latter category is made up of every company who is *not a part* of Amazon themselves. If you have your own eCommerce store, this is you. Now, several of these third-party businesses are going to be selling the same product, with the same details listed on their site. The sellers then, compete to win the "Buy Box", because, with this option on your page, you become the seller whose product is selected. Your product becomes the one customers add to their cart or buy now. 83% of sales on Amazon happen through the Buy Box option, which makes it a statistic you cannot ignore. In addition, yes, you have to "win" this option and it is Amazon who determines who the winner is. Amazon relies on an algorithm, which then determines the seller who will be represented in the Buy Box and for what duration. One thing's for sure, the Buy Box is going to give you a lot of preference as an FBA seller.

Chapter 7 Mistakes to Avoid

Not creating expandable brands and product lines from the start: If you are planning to build a sustainable business brand, you will want a larger umbrella of products to expand your business in the long run. Pick primary products that have plenty of complimentary purchases or can be bundled together with other items. This way you can keep adding items to create a longer product line under your brand. For example, if you zero in on the electronic gadgets niche, you may have a whole bunch of accessories and replaceable parts to sell to under a single business brand.

Go with bundled products and multi-packs if you are looking to score really big with Amazon FBA. Single items that sell are unlikely to be competition free or low competition on Amazon. Almost all products that sell reasonably well have tons of merchants in the category. Also, profit on one item products is swallowed by Amazon fees. Unless you can find a sweet spot between a high priced product that is also in demand and has low competition, you may not be able to achieve stellar results with single items.

Also, your woes will increase if Amazon sells the product. Unless you have a terrific edge, it is going to be hard to compete with Amazon. Bundling up products or creating multi-packs may require greater time or money. You need to source a variety of items and bundle them. However, it can be highly beneficial for long term profits.

Underestimating the holidays: As long as you are comfortable holding on to these items for roughly 10 months, the deals you can find on decorations during the days immediately after most major holidays can practically guarantee acceptable profit margins on nearly everything you can imagine. What's more, by waiting 10 months before sending them to Amazon, you minimize your storage costs while at the same time taking advantage of all the people who like to plan for the holidays early. Alternately, you can wait until just a few weeks prior to the holiday to post your products and raise the prices even more to grab customers who waited until the last second and as a result, don't care about the costs.

Another good place to look is in the autocomplete results of search engines on websites like eBay or Etsy, places where people are already going to search for harder to find items. In fact, if you ultimately find that the community for buying and selling related items is particularly robust, you may wish to consider starting a store on one of these platforms yourself.

Not listing products the right way

Even though we are told time and time again not to judge a book by its cover, shopping on Amazon, and anywhere online in general, is quite the opposite. One of the vital aspects of any listing on Amazon is the title, which informs potential buyers what the product is all about.

- Add keywords to the title to help the product to rank when buyers search
- Incorporate brand name
- Incorporate the name of the product Add any features that distinguish the item
    - Its use
    - Color
    - Size

For instance, if you are selling a pacifier, an ideal title would look something similar to this: Deluxe Silicone Baby Pacifier – Easy for Parents – BPA Free – Set of 2 Pacifiers – Blue

Goals for an Amazon product title should do the following:

- Educate potential consumers about the product, even before they read the product page
- Add a few keywords to showcase the product and its use

Not taking full advantage of images: Another important aspect of the product details of items on Amazon is the images included in the listing. They can cause shoppers to click on your listing just because of the quality of the image. That's why you should spend a good amount of time to research images that are top-notch. Amazon productimages should include:

- Showcase product size by having a human hold it
- Information images like charts
- Images that include features of the product and compare it to other similar items
- Images of your product being utilized
    - The back label
- The item from all different angles

A great resource to find top-notch Amazon images for your listings that are also affordable is AMZDream.com.

Not using enough bullet points: If potential buyers fail to be swooned by your choice of title and images, bullet points are the next best thing to get a straightforward reaction. You have five spaces to include bullet points, but this doesn't mean you only have to use five words or even sentences. I personally use short paragraphs in each of those bullet points to home in on benefits and features of the item. Address common questions and objections as well. Use the first three points to showcase your products most pertinent features and use the other bullet points to answer common inquiries or customer objections.

Not pricing products properly: Opt to sell private label products that are priced above $10. Amazon lists items priced below $10 as "Add On Items, which means buyers cannot purchase your item by itself. They have to make additional purchases to be able to buy your product. Additionally, profit margins for products priced below $10 after deducting Amazon's fee can be rather low for building a lucrative, long-term business. You will need a very higher sales volume to witness recent returns. Ideally, pick products that sell in the range of $10-$30 for higher profit margins.

Few things will kill you like low cost products on Amazon unless you predict an unrealistically high sales volume. You may think inexpensive items carry less risk or are more frequently picked up by customers on impulse. However, selling products for below $5 is not likely to be profitable even with a high sales volume or next to nothing sourcing price. The shipping cost (to Amazon's warehouse) and fees

will leave you with a few pennies.

Not treating it like a business: While Amazon FBA is not the same as having your traditional website up and running where you sell products to people, you should still treat the time that you spend on Amazon FBA the same that you would like an e-commerce business. Even though using Amazon FBA allows you to move away from creating your website, this does not mean that you should not take Amazon FBA seriously. You can lose money through this platform if you're not accurate in your estimates or you're sloppy with your profit margin calculations.

Not doing enough research: Another tip that many Amazon FBA users miss is that they don't do research on the Amazon site itself before deciding which products they're going to sell. Even if you enjoy fishing, this does not necessarily mean that selling fishing poles on Amazon is a decision that is going to lead to profits. Look at what's selling the most frequently on Amazon, and take note of any markets that may look like they're being underrepresented.

Having too many similar products: Unlike the notion of a niche website that we've already discussed, you do not have to worry about keeping a product line that is similar when you're using Amazon FBA. Because your seller profile is not going to define the type of business that you're running, you have the freedom to pick and choose the products that you want to sell. This can be great for someone who is good at doing research on products within Amazon's website. By figuring out the profit margin that's possible from certain products that are on the market, you should be able to make better financial decisions for yourself and your business.

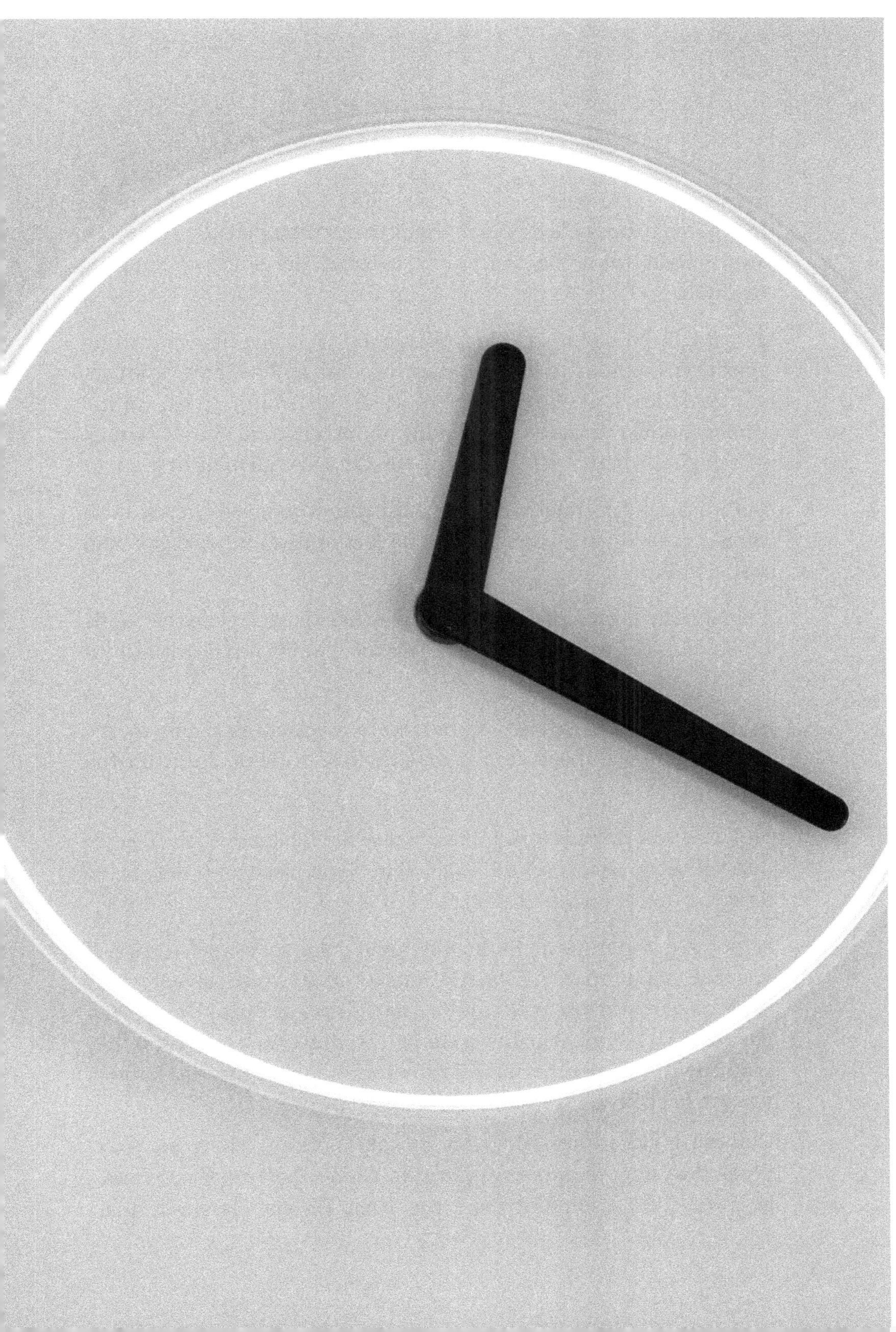

Chapter 8 Delays

In regards to possible delays, it is fair to mention that you should be aware right from the beginning, even at the stage of supplier research.

You might be having a Friday afternoon, and feel like contacting your first suppliers to see how they respond, and you might not get any reply for a week from any of them. Instead of giving up the whole supplier research or thinking about what did you do wrong, you might be better-off looking up the Chinese calendar first.

In China holidays might differ according to where you live, and you should not only be aware, but also understandwhat they mean, and respect that.

I personally even write them messages like; have a good rest while on holiday and to all Factory workers too, but it's not necessarily at all.

Some of these holidays are not really chosen, but due to the Government, it's been forced on everyone to shut down all the factories.

Holidays can cause issues at both end of the Businesses, the factory and you as an Amazon FBA seller. When you place an order, make sure you don't run out of stock.

As you see sometimes, production might delay for a week or two. If you are not prepared properly, once you have no inventory at Amazon, you will lose your ranking, as well as loose profit, and many customers who might go buy a similar product. And next time they may buy the same other brand rather than look for you to know if you are back in stock.

Chinese holidays are important to take note of. There are also times that huge events take place in China that you should also be aware of, as some of them can even kill your business like many Amazon FBA sellers experienced when the Olympics took place in China in 2008.

The pollution is very high in China, so anytime a big event takes place, the Government takes extra measures by closing most factories in order to have a better looking sky.

It doesn't really matter where you source from, however you should watch the news and understand external causes of possible delays.

In regards to AIR shipping there are few days of delays that I have experienced, literally 1 or 2 days. It happened with DHL, as the Duty had to be paid before delivery, and I had to reschedule the delivery. I wasn't able to reschedule for Saturday, so I had to wait from Friday till Monday, knowing that my product was sitting at DHL's ware house since the Friday afternoon instead of me actually doing my quality checks.

Sea shipping will always take at least 4-6 weeks, if you source from China to the US, and possible delays might take another week or two.

Also, when sourcing by Sea Shipping, same as Air Shipping, Duties must be paid before picking up your shipment, or sending a freight forwarder for collection, and that is the most convenient option.

Also when importing with Sea Shipping, there are some busy times where public holidays could cause port congestion and your shipment could be delayed.

Always communicate with your suppliers to avoid any possible delays, as you might not have experienced. However, your supplier might be able to suggest good times for shipping, since they may know more about local news and Shipping Agencies than you.

Clearance paperwork can also cause delay before your product is released. So it's a good idea to be ready with all the documents that is required for this purpose on time, and make sure there are no errors on any of the documentations that you will provide as all that might just cause you additional delays.

In a perfect situation, to be able to source from any country to another should take no time, however there are so many steps, and so many companies are involved that for most of them you or your supplier are not special at all, and if they find something incorrect or against their procedure, it will cause a great loss of money to your Business.

Chapter 9 Frequently Asked Questions

What does Fulfillment by Amazon represent?

Fulfillment by Amazon (FBA) is a very interesting option provided by this platform, which can help merchants boost their business by taking advantage of Amazon's expertise and resources, fast, free and trustworthy shipment, and outstanding customer support services. By choosing this option, you can send your inventory to the platform's warehouses (fulfillment centers) so that they can be stored over there and then leave everything to Amazon, including the picking, packing, and shipping of your customers' orders.

FBA is eligible for all the product categories and subcategories showing up on the Amazon Seller account. It is also available for any reseller who is curious to try it. The maximum weight limit for this program is 30 kilograms per product, so this is a requirement you need to know right from the start. You can test how your products are selling on Amazon, as well as send plenty of them to the fulfillment centers because you don't have to pay for anything upfront. You merely have to spend on their services that you use at the end of the month or when you make a sale.

What exactly is the Amazon Seller Central?

When selecting the selling plan, you should be able to see the prices of both plans easily. The Individual account costs $0.99, while the Professional one amounts to $39.99. These are both monthly fees, and you are charged 30 days after the registration process.

Is it possible to create an Amazon Selling account for free?

Unfortunately, this is not an option on this platform because you need to choose between an Individual or Professional account.

What do I have to do in order to comply with Amazon's return policy?

Amazon will ask you to provide the following methods for returns:

- a return address;
- a prepaid return level; and
- a full refund without asking for the product to be returned.

How do consumers recognize the Fulfillment by Amazon products on the platform?

These products have the "Fulfillment by Amazon" logo, which provides the customers with the information that support service, returns, packing, and delivery are handled by Amazon.

How to label individual products?

When you wish to add your listings on the platform, you will be faced with a decision that can influence your further success on Amazon. To be precise, you have to select the labelling option, whether you want to send the products using EAN or UPC barcodes (these products fall into the Commingled Inventory or Stickerless category), or label the products properly (Labeled Inventory) to hide the original barcode completely. Commingled Inventory can be combined with other inventories from different merchants; that's why your customers might get products from different resellers, which may or may not have the same features as yours. Amazon will not open the boxes to check which product is the right one and from which merchant it has come from to ensure the authenticity of the merchandise. The Stickerless option, on the other hand, only refers to the products, not to the delivery. Although it may be a bit time- consuming and complicated, you may need to label the items well to protect your inventory and make sure that your customers are getting what they have ordered.

How to print labels for your own products?

When you are adding new products (inventory) from your Seller Central account (you will need to go into "Inventory Amazon Fulfils" and then "Send/replenish inventory") or just preparing an inventory, you are entering something called "shipping workflow." It will provide extra guidance on how to prepare your inventory to be shipped to Amazon's warehouses, thus giving you the option to customize the shipment considering the selections that you make during each step. At one point, you will be prompted to choose the labelling option and allow you to print your unit labels from the shipping workflow directly. These tags will include details like the product title, which can prove to be very helpful when it comes to matching the label with the right product. You need a printer and blank adhesive papers to print such labels, which can be found on the Amazon website or any store that sells office supplies.

Is there a possibility for Amazon to add the labels on your products?

This is a possible option, especially when you are entering the shipping workflow guide. You can simply select Amazon Label Service when prompted with the labelling options. This is a valid solution if you find the private label process too complicated and time-consuming.

How to pack products when sending them to Amazon?

You can find two different types of packing products before sending them to Amazon's warehouses below.

- Individually packed goods means that every box contains one or few units, depending on conditions and quantities.
- Packing items in a case is an option that will allow the

merchant to place the products with the same SKU and condition into one box. The boxes will have the same quantity and the same item in them. When Amazon receives these boxes, they will only scan one item from the box and place the whole thing in your inventory. Amazon does not need to scan all the items, considering they are all the same.

When the reseller sends the products to Amazon, they can only be sent using one type of packing per shipment. Although they will be added to the inventory, if the merchant has individually packed items and cases with packed items, he or she will need to send them separately to Amazon.

How to choose a shipping method and carrier to send your inventory to Amazon?

The starting point of creating a new shipment is the "Send/replenish inventory" tab, which is present in the "Inventory Amazon Fulfils" section of your account. It is also possible when you have a work-in-progress inventory and you use the "shipping workflow" tool. By using the latter, you will receive step-by-step instructions on how to prepare your merchandise to be sent over to Amazon, including details about customizing your shipment according to the selections that you make at each step. One of them will allow you to choose from the shipping methods below:

- Small Parcel Deliveries (SPDs) represent individually packed and labelled products (one product per box), all prepared to be shipped.
- Less-Than-Truckload (LTL) shipments are, in fact, a mixed delivery because it contains pallets and individually boxed products. In this case, some of the products may be sent to different

destinations, different warehouses.

- Full Truckload (FTL) also combines full pallets and individually packed products. The difference, however, is that the whole merchandise is going to one warehouse.

The FBA terms and conditions apply to all products that you send to and are meant to be sold on Amazon, regardless of the shipping method that you select. You can find more details related to how the platform receives and routes your products if you check these terms and conditions.

You can also choose a different carrier, other than the one provided by Amazon. Costs can be higher in this case, but if you do want to go ahead with this option, you will need to work with a trusted carrier that is capable of providing you with valuable information like a valid tracking number for SPD, the pro/freight bill number for FTL or LTL deliveries, and the bill of lading (BOL).

You can't send the inventory to Amazon using a privately- owned car, however. It can only be done by a registered carrier.

How to create shipping labels?

The shipping workflow is a sequence and tool where you can simply choose the type of labels that you want to have (if there is any). When selecting Small Parcel Delivery (SPD), you will be prompted to print shipping labels (just one per box) and packing slips. You will also need to place the packing slip inside the box, on the top side, so that it can be seen immediately after being opened at the Amazon's warehouse. The information that you should include are the destination and return addresses, while the label should be positioned just outside the sealed box as an addition to labels added by the carrier.

If you select Less-Than-Truckload, you still need to print a label per each box, which has to be placed outside of it so it can be seen when unwrapping the pallet. On the pallets, the tags have to be placed in a top-center position on each side (on the stretched wrap).

Adhesive labels can be found at any office supplies store or on Amazon.

Is it possible to arrange a shipment of inventory directly from an overseas supplier?

This is not an acceptable option because Amazon can't be used as the final address, importer or consignee when sending products from overseas. In this case, merchants will have to make the necessary arrangement to import and clear the shipment of customs. Only after doing this that they can send the inventory to Amazon's warehouses.

How to notify Amazon in advance regarding the products that I'm sending to them?

You have three options of sending products over to Amazon: Small Parcel Delivery (SPD), Less-Than-Truckload (LTL), and Full Truckload (FTL). For the last two choices, you will need to arrange delivery appointments; otherwise, the fulfillment centers may decline your shipment. In order to arrange a delivery appointment with the warehouse where you want to send the inventory, you will need first to download the Fulfillment by Amazon booking form, fill it, and email it to the carrier. In this form, you will have to place the ZIP code (you can find it in the Shipping Queue section of your account). Once the carrier has received your form, they will send it to the Amazon's Fulfillment Center to schedule the best delivery timing. It usually takes around 24 hours for the warehouse to reply back to the carrier with a confirmation for the delivery time.

VISA

Chapter 10 How to Find Profitable Products to Sell

The question of how to find profitable products to sell is one that depends heavily upon your preferred method of acquiring inventory. If you already have experience selling online and have the funds necessary to invest in your own line of products, head to the Private Labeling section for an in-depth description of the process.

If this is your first time venturing into online sales and you are looking for a quick easy way to get some experience selling and make a sizable supplementary profit, retail arbitrage is the name of the game.

After you've gotten comfortable using the scanner, it is time to hit the streets looking for those discounted and clearance items. The most important thing to address here is to find products for sale at a discount. At the same time, the product also needs to be able to sell. If it doesn't sell quickly enough, it will sit in the warehouses racking up fees. So, how do you know if an item will sell well?

Amazon Ranking System

Amazon uses its own raking system to categorize the products on its website. By looking at this ranking system, you can figure out how well an item sells. Items with lower numbers sell more quickly, which means more of them are bought on a daily basis. An item's ranking in included in the product description.

The Amazon Ranking System is important to understanding how the business of FBA works. First of all, know that a product's rank is based on its sales. It does not take into account reviews or ratings. This is not to say reviews and ratings are not useful; they can be encouraging for people to buy your items, which is how they ultimately contribute to the ranking a product earns. Sales are evaluated relative to other products in a category, so the ranking is not about the quantity of items sold.

Ranking plays an important role for all products sold on Amazon, but particularly for books, it becomes crucial to be aware of the item rank. If you are not selling books, it is important for different reasons. If you are looking at a product ranking for retail arbitrage, you are aiming for an item with a rank lower than 50,000 in its category. For private label, 12,000 is a better goal. The problem with sales rankings is that they cannot tell you everything about how an item will sell. They change over time and are based on the most recent sale period, so they are not necessarily reflective of an item's overall selling potential.

When you are looking to sell an item, you want to be sure that is desirable for the customer, but also that the competition is not too stiff to break into. To better get a sense of the accuracy of the sales rank, check out the reviews it has. If an item has many reviews and a good rank, you know that its rank is a result of sustained performance and not just a temporary jump.

If you are concerned about the rank of the product you are selling, refer to the section of this guide on Amazon Pay-Per- click (PPC) advertising, a sure-fire way to improve the visibility, and thus selling potential, of your product.

Amazon Guidelines

There are some products that cannot be sold through Amazon FBA. Counterfeit products are not allowed. You can check Amazon's restricted product list to figure out which items are disallowed by Amazon; some are not completely disallowed, but restrictions are placed upon them. A few examples from the list of restricted products include: alcohol, food and beverage, tobacco and drug paraphernalia, weaponry, make-up and skin care items, medical products, animals, electronics, services, and art. For a complete and up-to-date list with specific information on restrictions, it is advisable to visit Amazon's official website for more information.

If you are interested in getting approval for items that are restricted to sell on Amazon (for example, beauty products or foodstuffs), you will need to register with a professional account. Then, you will need to seek approval by submitting no less than 3 paper invoices from authorized wholesale suppliers in reasonable quantities (at least 200 units). Retail arbitrage will not work for getting approval to sell unauthorized products; you will need an established business.

Chapter 11 Selecting the Right Product to Sell

How Can You Find the Right Product to Sell on Amazon?

Finding the right product to sell on Amazon may not be the most straightforward task, considering selling something that you like may already be sold by others. After all, you are in this game for the profit. To achieve your objectives, you may need to go the extra mile to discover the hidden secrets of selling on this global platform.

The ideal product to be sold on Amazon needs to have high demand associated with low competition to ensure that it isn't sold by many merchants. This is common sense since your goal is to find a niche that meets such a requirement. Having your private label can be a considerable advantage in this case, too, because you can mark your place in the market. You can then go after the potential customers without being bothered by competitors.

In this chapter, you can find all the necessary details related to products, which can get jaw-dropping high profits, how to conduct market research, how to test your competition, and which bestseller categories are on Amazon. When hundreds of millions of products are being sold on this platform, choosing the right goods to advertise can prove to be a challenging task. That's why you have to know exactly what you are looking for in the Amazon catalogue. By respecting the general guidelines, you can also find the best products to sell.

How to Recognize a Good Product?

What is the ideal product to sell on Amazon? How does it look like? What are the main characteristics you need to consider when choosing a merchandise? These are only a few questions to ask yourself at the beginning of this process. Regarding the latest question, you can find some key information on how to recognize the best product.

Affordable retail price, usually between $25 and $50

According to recent studies, this price range is big enough to cover fees on Amazon related to storage, fulfillment, and advertising. This is when you have high sales, and the volume of sales can easily cover all these expenses and guarantee a handsome profit. If the price is above $50, then many of the customers will no longer consider its attractiveness, and the rate of the goods is what people see. Hence, the purchases will drop significantly.

Very low seasonality

Meaning, the ideal outcome is not influenced by season fluctuation of sales. You need a product that can generate profits throughout the whole year, not just during a specific season.

Lesser reviews for the top sellers

Usually, 200 is good value in this case. However, less than 100 would be even better.

Room for improvement

You can analyze the feedback received from the customers and improve your product based on them.
Easy manufacturing

Such a product has to be easily manufactured and made of resistant materials; thus, you probably need to avoid glass. You also have to keep it simple. So, electronics and sophisticated goods are some examples of the things you should avoid.

Of course, these are just guidelines since your ideal product may be different from the other merchants. It's all about knowing exactly what to sell in the niche you choose to conduct your business.

Finding Products Fast and Easy

By this moment, you know what to look for in the massive database of the Amazon platform. However, you will need some proper tools to help you in this challenging mission. You need to find measurable information related to products, such as demand, price, seasonality, sales, rating, dimensions, price, and many more.

The Jungle Scout Web App can come in handy to help you scan the products from the platform using the Product Database extension. Another exciting feature is the Product Tracker, which can enable you to track inventory, sales activity, rankings, and prices over some time.

To make up your mind regarding the products to sell on Amazon, you need to track them for a few weeks before deciding after viewing the report provided by the Product Tracker feature. By doing so, you can get a clear idea about how the product performs. If you want to find a suitable niche with a high demand, a handy tool can be the Niche Hunter feature of the Jungle Scout Web App. This extension analyzes the most frequent keywords to discover in-demand goods. It can display a list with plenty of products that buyers search for as well. Furthermore, the feature provides an Opportunity Score, which is based on a search algorithm called Listing Quality Score (LQS). It is responsible for identifying the products with high demand and extremely low listing. The higher the Opportunity Score is, the better.

The Jungle Scout Web App can also be used with the Google Chrome extension to test a multitude of keywords. This process can also display some impressive results from which you can easily find out the competition levels for many products. Using all these tools, you can come up with a list of 20 products which fit all of your requirements, but these products will have to be tested.

Comprehensive Market Research

Once you made up your mind regarding the products you want to sell, the first question you need to ask yourself is: "How many items can I sell during a month?" The goods which have to be filtered by this query have to respect the following requirements.

Proper Sales Distribution

Meaning, one or two merchants do not dominate the niche market. Instead, the sales are distributed amongst a few sellers

Satisfactory Demand

Satisfactory demand is considered when the most active sellers on this market can easily sell at least ten items per day.

If you can generate ten sales per day or 300 per month, that's an outstanding figure to start with on Amazon. Jungle Scout extension can help you with this research since it can easily display a report after typing a few relevant keywords. Aside from the top merchandisers, it will also inform you of their sales volume, product prices, item demand, and many more.

Test Your Competition

After you have shortlisted the products that you want to sell, the second question to ask is: "What is the competition selling this item for?" Again, the Jungle Scout app can come in handy since it can show you some fascinating information like reviews and score ratings. The reviews are the most important aspect think about when analyzing your competitors since the number can give you a distinct idea about the size of the competition. A high number of review indicates a very competitive market - the kind of category you have to stay away from.

Moreover, the tool can also show you a list of products on demand that have a small number of reviews. This information is pure gold because that is what you need to get into. Excellent opportunities are usually referred to highly demanded products with less than 200 reviews; when we're talking about less than 100 studies, these are unique chances. To do your homework properly when assessing competition, you may need to read its reviews to improve your products before selling them as well. Furthermore, you can use the Jungle Scout app to establish which items will be your secondary products. These are the goods that you can still get some profits out of, but you may need to track the results for at least a week or two. By doing so, you are already one step ahead of your competitors.

Also, when studying your competition, it matters to think about a significant feature: Amazon Best Seller Ranking. To explain this term simply, it refers to the order the products that are being listed on a page. The platform sorts and arranges every merchandise that was sold at least once into a hierarchy, which is the Best Seller Ranking (BSR). Using this indicator and the Jungle Scout sales estimator tool you can roughly calculate the product sales volume of your competitors. To be specific, you can choose the category, the marketplace, enter the BSR, and obtain their sales estimation. Such a tool can provide you with the right information to become one step in front of your competition once you apply the proper strategies and get the expected results. If the items that you are selling only have a few reviews, you can seriously play a significant role in this market niche after making some sales.

To be successful on Amazon, you will need to sell the right products. To make that happen, you have to be extremely practical and sell what is in high demand and has high chances to be sold. It does not necessarily have to be what you like because there may be plenty of other merchants desiring the same product. Furthermore, you might face a steep competition with more established sellers if you insist on doing so. You also have to be incredibly passionate about the products you are selling because you need to know everything about every merchandise to provide the information that the customers need to see, as well as to improve its quality. That is one way for you to create a well- appreciated brand, which the consumers will want to trust and buy from again.

Best Selling Categories on Amazon

One good starting point to select the right products to sell on this platform is to check the statistics of the bestselling categories and sub-categories. The good news is that it's the kind of information that can readily be found on the Amazon website. Therefore, you can browse through the site's categories and wait for each one to display the best sellers. If you limit your search on the specific sections, you will find the best-selling merchants, who may also be extremely competitive; that's why tackling them may not be the wisest thing to do.

However, if you go further and browse through the sub-categories, you may come across best sellers that are worth your efforts. Some products are merely better sold under a private brand, but the areas that may be for everyone are:

- kitchen and dining
- pet supplies
- sports and outdoors
- patio, lawn, and garden
- home and kitchen

Chapter 12 Ordering Product from Suppliers

You now have a list filled with excellent possibilities for products that you could be selling in your shop, which means that you are ready to start sourcing these products so that you can move on to actually selling them! Ordering products tend to be the most daunting part of the entire business, as this is the part where you are taking the biggest risk in your Amazon FBA business. When it comes to ordering products, you are now relying on the idea that these products are going to sell out and you are going to earn a profit from them have sold. If it did not work out in your favor, you could be out a large amount of money and in possession of many products that you do not want to have any longer.

This means that at least some of the stress should be taken off and that you can start settling into the idea that you are going to be successful, because you are using a winning guideline for how you can earn money using Amazon FBA.

In this chapter, you are going to go through important series of finding suppliers and qualifying them for your business. You are also going to learn about how you can place your order, and when it is the right time to pull the trigger on placing your order. This way, you can feel confident that you have ordered your products properly and at the right time.

Selecting Possible Suppliers for Amazon FBA

The first thing that you need to do is create a list of possible suppliers that you might consider for stocking your Amazon

FBA shop with. At this point, you can easily begin to identify possible suppliers by doing a Google search on suppliers who offer a particular product that you are looking for. When it comes to looking for suppliers you want to look at both wholesalers and manufacturers, as both are going to be able to offer the services that you need to stock your Amazon FBA shop. Avoid shopping through other retailers as their markups are going to be excessive for this particular purpose, since their products are priced for consumers and not businesses who want to purchase large quantities.

As you look for suppliers, be sure to jot down possible suppliers next to every single product that you are considering selling in your store. This way, you can have access to their information for reference when you begin to qualify the suppliers, which will make it easier for you to compare them against one another and validate their quality. Ideally, you want to have 2-3 suppliers per product variety to ensure that you are going to have plenty to choose from. If you have only one, you can still jot it down, but it may not measure up during the qualifying process, which means that you may have a lower chance of stocking that particular item unless your possible supplier is high quality.

After you have found all of the possible suppliers who can help you stock your shop, you want to start writing down important information about each supplier. Think of all of the information that would be relevant to you purchasing their products, and use that to help you create comparison charts. You want to consider how expensive their products are, what their minimum order quantity is, how expensive shipping is, how long it takes for their products to arrive after being shipped, and how they handle quality control complaints. You also want to consider where they are located, as this might contribute to how easy or difficult they are to communicate with. If a company is located overseas, it may indicate that they will be more challenging to communicate with due to the language and cultural barriers that you both face. That being said, overseas companies do tend to produce cheaper goods, so consider the quality of the written content on their website to identify how easy they are to interpret. If their written content is incredibly low or poorly translated, it may indicate that they are going to be harder to communicate with and that you might run into troubles with communication. If their written content seems easy to interpret and well written, chances are they will be easier to communicate with which will make your job easier when you choose to work with them.

With your comparison charts completed, take a moment to disqualify obvious non-contenders. This means any company who is going to be too expensive to shop through, any company with low-quality shipping services, or any company who might be too challenging to communicate with should be disqualified. At this point, there is no reason to further research these particular companies as possible suppliers, if you can already tell that they are not offering what you are looking for.

Qualifying Suppliers and Their Products

Any suppliers that have made it past the obvious disqualifications on your comparison charts are now ready to enter the qualifying stage. This is where you are going to qualify both suppliers and their products to determine which company is going to offer the highest quality of products and services for what you are looking for. This part of the process can be lengthy as you are going to be researching and testing several different companies to ensure that the products that you are going to be stocking are high quality and are coming from great suppliers.

The first step in qualifying a supplier is to make contact with them. As you make contact with the supplier, message them to let them know that you are interested in considering their products for your shop. You can also ask questions such as how long shipping typically takes, what shipping methods they use, how early you should order products when you need to restock, and what their minimum quantity orders are. Even if these types of questions are already answered on the website, make sure to ask them in the email as well. In doing so, you gain the opportunity to see how well they communicate and whether or not they offer positive service when you are inquiring about doing business with them. At this point, some suppliers might take a long time answering, or they might answer in a way that is difficult to understand or that suggests that there will be great difficulty in overcoming language or cultural barriers when you are purchasing with them. This does not mean that they are a bad supplier, but it does mean that you might have difficulty communicating with them to deal with any possible needs or issues that you may face along the way.

Once you have received information back from a possible supplier and you have scored the quality of service and communication that they have offered, you want to move on to ordering samples from them. Ideally, you should order one sample of every single product that you are considering buying from them, so that you can get a hands-on feel for the quality of that product. This is your primary opportunity to engage in quality control on the physical products that you are considering selling, so it is incredibly important. Do not rely on reviews and probability here: *always test the product.* If you do not, you might risk having a low-quality product for sale that could do great damage to your reputation as well as cost you significantly in returned orders or inability to move product. *Do not skip this step.*

At this point, you have effectively established a personal opinion on suppliers and you have validated the quality of their products. The last step before committing to a supplier is doing additional research to see what you can learn about that supplier. Remember: sometimes, salespeople will do and say; everything they need to in order to get you to purchase from them, but then the quality of service goes downhill from there. This does not mean that everyone will do this, but some businesses are guilty of it and if you are caught in this, it can leave you in a huge deficit with your products. The best way to avoid this is to look for external evidence that the supplier you have chosen is going to be able to offer high-quality products and service. You can do this by looking for external reviews on their company, which can be done by either Googling their company for reviews, or by joining social media groups and online forums devoted to e- commerce. In these areas, you can find reviews by real people who have actually worked with that particular company to see what the truth is about that particular company. This way, you can identify any possible issues beforehand in order to avoid being caught in an unwanted situation with expensive products on hand.

When and How to Place Your Order

You should now feel confident in who are planning to order your products from, and which products you are going to be stocking your store with for your launch. Now, you need to know how to determine when you should place your order and what needs to happen for your order to be placed. When it comes to Amazon FBA, the way that orders are placed are slightly different and do require more steps, so be sure to pay close attention to this part to ensure that you are following the steps correctly. Doing this incorrectly could lead to an expensive mistake where Amazon ships your products back to the supplier because they were not properly registered, which you would then have to pay for. You would also have to pay again for your products to be shipped back to Amazon, which could result in three possible charges as opposed to one, which can be incredibly expensive on large shipments of stock.

The first thing you need to understand is that you do not have to order your products right away. In fact, you should not order your products just yet, as you will want to have some form of brand and audience in place before you begin launching products, therefore you have people to market your products to. So, until you begin engaging in organic social media marketing and building a small name for your brand, do not order products just yet. This proactive marketing is a crucial first step for E-Commerce businesses as this is how you establish your earliest crowd and begin to guarantee your earliest success. Ideally, you should have 500-1,000 people in your social media audience on your chosen primary platform before you begin to actually release products to anyone. This way, you have a strong, healthy audience filled with people who have already shown interest in the types of products that you are going to have available.

After you have an existing audience to launch to, you can submit your orders for your chosen products and start having them shipped to Amazon's warehouse. This way, you have your products ready to go for the launch date and you officially move your project into motion. At this point, you are making your launch a real thing and you are reaching the point of no return.

With ordering your products, you are going to have to fulfill your supplier's requirements and fulfill Amazon's requirements in order to purchase your products, and have them shipped to and accepted by Amazon's employees. You should start by approving your products in the Amazon backend, so that when you order your products from the manufacturer Amazon already approves them.

You can have your products approved on Amazon by signing into your Amazon Seller Central account and going to "Manage Inventory." There, you want to select "New Inventory" and then fill out all of the details about the new products that you are going to be stocking that will be sent to Amazon. What information is needed will depend on what types of products you are sending, so the best guidance to follow here is everything that you see on screen. Make sure that everything Amazon requests are filled out to the best of your ability. Be especially careful in uploading product SKUs into your product profile, as Amazon will deny any products that do not have the exact SKU that you have uploaded so despite tiny inaccuracy can turn out to be disastrous.

After you have registered your new product into your Amazon Seller Central account, you can go to your Manage Inventory page once again, highlight the chosen product, and click "Action on Selected" and then click "Send/Replenish Inventory." You will then be prompted to create a new shipping plan for the product that you are going to be shipping to the Amazon warehouse, so that Amazon's employees know what is happening with your shipment.

The first step in creating your shipping plan is confirming the ship-from address, which is the address of your supplier that will be shipping the products to Amazon. Make sure that you get this address correct because if there are any troubles with your shipment, Amazon is going to send it back to the manufacturer, and if the address is wrong, this could get even more expensive with a lost package.

Next, you need to confirm your packing type. Amazon offers two options to choose from individually packed or case packed. If you are going to be selling individual items, you are going to select individually packed as your packing type. If you are going to be selling multiples grouped together, you want to select case packed. For example, if you were going to sell one individual box of tea, you would select individually packed. However, if you were going to sell ten individual boxes of tea together as a case, you would select case packed. It is worth mentioning that if you are selling individual packages or cases; make sure to mention this to your suppliers so that they can package your products properly for Amazon.

With this information inputted, your basic shipping plan will be designed and now you will have to create the rest of the shipping plan for your package. You will click "Continue to Shipping Plan" and then you will need to select the preparation method. Either you can prepare a shipping plan yourself, or you can request that Amazon creates the shipping plan for you.

Then, you need to prepare and label your products, which will all be done through the systematic system built into Amazon FBA's platform. Next, you will set the quantity and print those labels as needed. Finally, you will preview your shipment, prepare your shipment, choose your shipment type, and then confirm your shipment.

Regarding choosing your shipment type there are two options: Small Parcel Delivery, or Less Than Truckload. Small Parcel Delivery would be anything coming in a single box. For this, you would input the weight and dimensions of each box and put that into your pack list. If you choose Less Than Truckload, this means you are getting a large number of boxes delivered, so you will need to indicate the number of boxes being delivered and enter all of the shipping information from your carrier into them.

Once you have confirmed all of this through Amazon FBA, you can confirm and finalize your order through your supplier. At this point, all you should need to do is purchase the quantity from your supplier and give them Amazon's warehouse address, which can be found in the information with your shipping plan. Then, your products should be shipped to Amazon and they should be managed according to your shipping plans instructions. Information about your shipment will be uploaded directly into your Amazon Seller Central account, where you will be able to see if the shipment has been received and how much stock you have with each product. At first, you should have the entire stock that you ordered, however as it begins to sell you will start seeing those numbers drop.

amazon
VS420274
VS420324
VS420324
azon
amazon

Chapter 13 Shipping

Now it's time to get your products shipped to their destination! There are a few things you should know right off the bat:

- Always make sure that the cost of customs clearance is included in a freight company's door- to-door service before placing orders overseas.
- Always get a quote in WRITING and make sure that is DDP (delivered duty paid). This means that the seller (not you) has to bear the risks and costs, including duties, taxes and other charges of delivering the goods to it, cleared for importation.
- Ask your supplier for a freight quote. Sometimes they have great relationships and could save you money on your shipments.
- Sometimes it's worth it to send about 20% of your shipment by Air Freight and the remaining 80% by Sea. This way, you don't pay that much more, you get your stock in much faster. This is great to do when:
    - You want to get started sooner; or
    - You're running out of stock, and you must receive it as soon as possible, or you will be out of stock for a long period.
- You must be certain that *all information supplied to the broker, air courier, or postal service is true and correct*. A power of attorney does not extend beyond their role as your Customs Broker. This is one rule you must learn. You are legally responsible for the facts declared in any declaration lodged for clearance purposes. Even if your broker makes an error, you are legally responsible. One area that few consider in this respect is declared value. It is almost universal practice for Asian suppliers to under-declare the

shipment value, or declare the goods as a gift, thinking they are doing you a favor. Chinese suppliers will do it routinely unless at the time of placing the order you firmly tell them not to. The majority of importers insist on them showing false values.

- You don't need to ship the product to you before shipping it to Amazon. We prefer shipping direct. Don't think for a second that your supplier doesn't know that your selling on Amazon and that they can't find your exact listing.

Basics of Shipping

Air shipping vs. Sea

- Air Shipping is usually split into
    - Air Freight – 15-20 days (door to door)
        - More expensive than sea freight
        - Dimensions and weight determine the price
        - Packing type is through cartons or palletized
        - Price will vary more than by sea depending on the period
        - Longer transit times (layovers) is usually cheaper than shorter transit times

- Express – 3 to 5 days (DHL, FedEx, UPS, etc...)
    - Mostly used for samples

- Sea
    - Good for Oversized Products or Bigger Orders
    - Will take 35-45 days

- Price is determined by dimensions/Volume (CBM – Cubic Meters)
- Packing type is LCL (Less than Container Load or Consolidation) / FCL (Full Container Load)
  - LCL
  - Best use for below 15cbm shipments
  - You'll share a container with others (sharing the fee)
  - More expensive vs. FCL
  - FCL
  - Different sizes to choose from
  - Safer if all the container goes to the same location

The Larger a product is, the more economical it will be to ship by sea. If it's very small, it may be cheaper to send through Air!

How/When to use Air shipments?

- Launching a new product and you want to get feedback faster (send 30% by air, and 70% by sea can be an option depending on a case by case basis)
- Air shipments are usually better than running out of inventory (a % by air and the rest by sea works as well in this case)

Using Sea shipments

- Extremely cost effective for larger and heavier shipments
  - Longer transit time (usually about 40 days from start to end)
    - About 15-20 days from port to port (China to LA) without the customs clearance

Better Management

- If you're shipping products from multiple

suppliers, try to consolidate all the products using your freight forwarder. This will improve your margins and save you time managing the shipments.

- Plan and be on the lookout for Chinese holidays
  - Prepare your production accordingly so you can save money on shipping. Shipping during high seasons will cost you more.
- Most of the time, try to avoid DHL, UPS, and FedEx – their cost will be much higher. Use a freight forward or check out the in the "Getting Quotes" section.

Evaluating different freight services for cost-effectiveness

Here I should add a note about cost-effectiveness because it can be too easy to think that the lowest freight cost per item is the one to choose. It may be, but that is not necessarilyso.

You should consider what is known as opportunity cost. Faster delivery means a quicker turnover of your capital, and can considerably reduce your capital cost. While I am not teaching business economics, I suggest you consider what it might cost you in lost earnings on the capital needed to pay for your goods while they are in transit. It may cost you interest payments, or it may lose interest that you could otherwise earn.

There is also the need to consider the lost sales and ranking that might result from the delay.

FBA Shipping Labels

Carton Labels

- They are FBA labels applied to the master carton.
- You will receive this label while you're creating

your shipment plan in Seller Central.

- Make sure that your Packing Type is "Case- packed products."
- If you're sending in a product with 2 different colors, you'll have to make sure that you don't mix any of the colors. If you fit 25 units in a carton and you're sending 500 units (250 blue and 250 red), you will need to have 10 cartons with 25 units of red and 10 cartons with 25 units of blue.
- Decide WHERE you want those cartons shipped. To your home, warehouse, directly to Amazon?

o There are pros and cons to all those methods. If you don't ship to Amazon directly, then you're spending more time and money to inspect and ship the products again.

- Those labels are only valid for 3 months. Send them right before the inspection or 1-2 weeks before the final production date.

Inspections

Getting your shipments inspected is a no-brainer. It's not that expensive and it can be the difference between thousands of dollars lost and the quality you were expecting. Is it the last line of defense (if you're shipping directly to Amazon) before your customers receive the product. You must do it before paying the 70% balance!

Most people don't want to pay for the inspection, here are a few reasons why you must do it:

- It's way cheaper and easier to fix the issue before you paid the remaining 70% balance to your supplier.
- Once you've received the product in EU or US, it's usually too late to do anything about it (in most cases).
- Some suppliers don't want the inspection company to visit their factories (big red flag)

- Freight can be quite expensive, so better make sure that the product is perfect before.
- They will replace the products that don't pass the inspection.

What should they look for?

- The inspection companies know the drill. Nonetheless, you should confirm with them exactly what they'll do before. You'll want them to do:
    - Carton drop test – 5 times at 3 feet high
    - Unit drop test – 2-3 feet high drop
    - Check your competitors' complaints list so that they can test against those key points
    - Verification of quantity, item weight, dimensions, packaging (printing, sturdiness), labels, made in China/PRC marking

Here is a list of the companies that I consider to be reliable:

- Bureau Veritas
- TUV Rheinland

- SGS
- Intertek
- Sinotrust
- KRT Audit Corporation (US based)
- Cotecna
- Topwin (Chinese service cheaper than others)

Getting Quotes

What information you need:

- Carton Size
- # of Cartons
- Gross Weight of shipment or per Carton
- Address of the warehouse where your product is (if shipping FOB)**
- Which port (if shipping FOB)**
- Make sure that the duty rate is included (and is the same in all your quotes so that you can compare them)

**Not necessary if you use to pay your freight through your supplier

I suggest you get a quote for both Sea and Air Freight so that you can compare the difference in pricing. Sometimes you could be surprised. Depending on the weight and size of your product, it will vary a lot.

Where to go to find your Quotes?

- https://www.flexport.com/
- https://freightos.com
- Ask your supplier
- Shop around, they are so many different freight forwarders out there

Both websites above are quite easy to use. You should be able to look at YouTube or directly contact them if you need help.

Inventory Management System

Having a system in place to ensure you don't run out of stock and have too much product on hand is crucial. First, you have to know:

- How many units per day on average you're selling (ASV – Average Sales Velocity)
  - We focus on the last 30 days, but will also look at the last 7 and 14 days to ensure it's still in line.
- You must always be able to answer "*How many days of inventory do I have left?*"
  - Also known as "Days on Hand."
  - It will be easily calculated: (Inventory on Amazon for product X / ASV of product X)
- *When will you need to reorder?* You must know your lead time
  - Lead time = Manufacturing time + Inspection time + Shipping Time
  - Reorder Time = Days on Hand – Lead Time – Safety Margin (14 Days)
  - The Safety Margin is there to minimize the risk of running out of stock
- *How much will you need to order?*
  - During Q4 (November – December will usually be 2-3x your regular ASV!)
    - It varies by category, but it will increase.
  - Reorder Quantity = ASV * 60-90 days
    - We like to order between 60 to 90 days of inventory per order.

○ You can also ask your manufacturer to hold onto 30-45 days of inventory in case you need to send in stock faster than you think. This will also save you storage fees.

Chapter 14 Tips for Success

Free inventory from your house: In my house, and likely yours as well, there are those items that you have not been used, ever! Not since you bought it because it was on sale, or there was a discount on the commodity. You could have used it once and return to the furthest corner of your closet or kitchen cabinet; no matter the case, these items can be turned into cash or better, profit! All you have to do is ship them to Amazon for that to happen.

Go hunting! Look through your book shelves, not all books in your library you like them, get them out and create space for the series you have been dying to read in your house and also reduce clutter. Go into your cabinets in your kitchen, your kids (if you have any) rooms with their permission, of course, your room as well and get rid of anything that you do not use at all. Some items you can get will surprise you; as these items can be used to create profits on Amazon.

Take the initiative and involve your family, friends, and neighbor-if they are willing to do so-and use all these items to earn cash! It can be an excellent way to spend a weekend, go through your trash to make money.

Using dunnage for shipments: The stuff, either puffy or protective wrapper, which you use to wrap your load to protect them from touching the sides of your shipping box that is the definition of dunnage.

There are various things you can use to protect your items so that they can arrive safely to your customer without breakage. The commodities in the list below are things you are most likely going to have in your house already. You can use:

- A newspaper blanket

- A variety of small cardboard boxes for glass items

- From your online arbitrage purchases, you can use the air pillows in them

- Tie printed papers in your everyday plastic grocery bags. This is to protect your shipment from getting in contact with the newsprint.

Free boxes from grocery stores for shipment: At the beginning of your Amazon FBA business, there won't be the need for you to pay for delivery boxes as you might not have the cash for it or you want to save the money you have for something else. You can get shipping boxes for free from grocery stores, your neighbors who have moved recently, or your friends or colleagues that have moved as well as places that recycle their old boxes. This will save you tons of cash. Make sure you select the best boxes out of all those that are at your disposal.

From the grocery store, ask the employees or attendees when they are restocking their shelves if you can have some of the boxes they are using. They are likely to let you come and collect to your heart's content or even when they are restocking come and get the boxes from their aisles.

Lighter fluid to remove price stickers: When reusing shipment boxes, there is the likelihood of price stickers being on them. Removing them is one struggle you will have to endure if you are trying to save money, but getting rid of the sticker residue is another struggle all on its own. When it comes to dealing with the residue from price stickers lighter fluid will do the trick every time.

Be careful when handling the liquid, and this will guarantee the removal of the residue. The process is quite simple, and all you will require is a Scotty peeler to remove the labels. You can use a

Ronsonol lighter fluid. To do this, you will:

- Pour some of the lighter fluid on the sticker residue you want to get rid off
- Wait for a few minutes, approximately 5 minutes before you can try and remove the labels
- Using your Scotty peeler, gently try and pry the tag off.

Free inventory from Freecycle.org: Join a group of your area on Freecycle Network to be able to see what people are getting rid of or giving away for free that you can use for your shipments. You might be shocked by the number of things that you can source using this network. I got board games- both used and new-; books, in boxes; kitchen appliances, among other things.

The way it works is:

- Claim an item on the Freecycle Network
- The owner will leave it on the front porch or sidewalk
- Go and collect your item!

And that's it! Fairly easy and straightforward. This makes it easy for you to coordinate with the owner as you will get to set a time that you will pass by to collect it.

Boxes from arbitrage purchases: To be honest, most of the sourcing that you do for this type of business is through online sourcing. This means that there will be shipments sent to you in boxes. Thus you can use these same boxes for your shipments to Amazon. But you have to go to be careful and remove all bar codes. This can be removed or covered up before you can use the UPS label or Amazon.

Productivity tools: There are times when you just need to have a nap without worrying over unnecessarily about the way your online store is doing or how the shipments are fairing or remember if you sent a reply to your customer's comment. Below are some productivity tools that can help you shave off some of that time:

- IFTTT (If This Then That): This is mainly used by sellers on Amazon or eBay. The app is used to alert the sellers of when sales have been made, or stock has been added back into inventory, or it has been added elsewhere.

- Facebook News Eradicator: With various sellers mainly spending their time on this social media platform going through the different FBA groups, it can take much of your time without you realizing it. To help you with this, this eradicator cuts down your extension extremely low. It allows you not to spend so much time on the internet getting to know what all your sources on Amazon

FBA are talking about or all seller community groups.

- Cleer Pro: is an online app for online arbitrage. It is a software that makes it easier for you as a vendor to browse easily when trying to look for deals, items or doing your research on Amazon.com

- Gmail Canned Responses: typing a similar response over and over again can get exhausting, and no one wants that kind of stress. Therefore, this app allows you to formulate a response that is going to reply automatically to the type of replies that come from your customers. The same app can be used to respond to an email you get in your Amazon seller inbox. Since Amazon allows you to use your email to respond to customers instead of creating a particular kind of email address, you can use this app.

    - Flashback Express: it can only be used on Windows, unfortunately. It can be used to quickly capture and annotate your voice and then upload the video on your screen. This can be used to communicate something that is in your store. Or deliver something that is on your screen to a colleague or your occasional customer. This makes the message more personal than ever, and it can be the best way to explain something to your customers in an easier manner, and it can make you quite popular among other clients. It can bring you more customers as well.

- Unroll.me: There are dozens upon dozens of emails that you receive from a seller on a daily basis about different offers that you are going to get from Amazon. The difference between having this app and not having it, is you are required to need to keep clicking delete or unsubscribe manually. This app allows you to unsubscribe from those emails or offers that you do not want to have in bulk. There are tutorials online that you can use to help you navigate through the app with ease.

Time saving hacks: To save your time as a salesperson when screening your items and scanning them, you can use the $0.00 buy cost to help you when browsing for items mainly in the app's field "Buy$." The time that you spend typing at the expense of the item is deducted since it costs nothing! You can use a calculator to subtract the actual buying price of the item from the profit price and decide on whether you will purchase the item or you will forgo it.

At times, it is not necessary for you to do the math of whether you will get to buy the product; all you have got to do is check if the price you are buying the item is higher or lower than the price of the profit you are bound to make.

An example would be if the cost of the head gear is at $12.99 and the profit you are required to make is at $9.99; you will not buy the item since it costs more than what you are going to get from the profit.

Other ways of reducing the scanning process are through downloading the Amazon 1Button app. It is an extension from chrome that shows you the price of the item you require, and it does the searching or looking or scanning for you.

An instance would be when looking for game boards; the app will let you know if the game is sold on Amazon and the price of the game. This saves you the trouble of going through Amazon trying to find the game and if it is even available and the price as well.

Keep in mind that not always does the search engine provide the results that you are looking for and at times the items might not even be available or found.

Make sure you invest in the best supplies you possibly can get your hands on. There are the common denominators of supplies that most Amazon sellers have in their arsenal and use them. Most of them swear by these items and can attest to their immense help when carrying out their daily sales.

Have a business credit card and checking account: in your daily life, you have a personal credit card that you use mainly to buy your items and spend it as you wish. You also, most definitely (if not, get one ASAP!) keep track of your expenses and savings as well.

You can have a software tracking app on your every expense charged to your credit card, be it personal or business. For the Amazon FBA, you need to have a business credit card and checking account to keep track of what you are spending on and where your money goes. This card and account need to be different from your credit and checking account.

You can use Quickbooks as a way to keep track of your personal and business accounts and credit cards. The app allows you to:

- Keep track of what you have spent
- Know how much you owe your credit card and
- Where you shop at

Run your business like a business: With this being your business, even if you are running it at your house, you need to run it like one. To make shipping easier, create your shipping and prepping station.

It doesn't have to be anything fancy or too elaborate, get a small table and lean it against a wall. Have drawers (they could be colored or whatever pattern you prefer) close by that house all your poly bags, shipping tapes, scissors, liquid fluid and any other necessary appliance that you need to wrap your shipping items and put them in your box.

Having or creating order in your house can help you run your business very smoothly. The station will help you reduce the time spent running around looking for scissors, the shipping tape or trying to figure out where to lay your merchandise at so that you can work.

The area around your working station can function as your prepping station, where you gather all your necessary items, put them together before you move to your working station to put the final touches on your product before shipping them off to your customer.

The station can act as a studio of some sort. When you have laid out your items on the table, you can take a picture of the items and use them for your store on Amazon. The pictures can be edited; changing the color in the background to pure white t put it on the product listing images section of your site.

Know a good deal when you see one: While finding a niche is important to the long term strength of your FBA store, the most important rule of FBA is that if you can make a profit on it then you should sell it. As such, regardless of what the product is if you find yourself staring at a sale that is 75 percent off or more then there is always going to be room enough there for you to make a profit on the item. The key to not putting too much work into this type of passive income is to always passively be on the lookout for good deals and be ready and able to jump on them when you see them because the best deals are never going to stick around for very long.

Care about your seller rating: Just because you letting Amazon do most of the heavy lifting doesn't mean that you can let your store run on autopilot. Specifically, you are going to want to be aware of your seller rating and do everything you can to keep it as high as possible. If you sell faulty merchandise or items that fall apart quickly then this number will drop rapidly which means you will want to consider all the costs of a particular product, not just what you pay to take direct ownership of the product. What's more, if you make a habit of selling unreliable items then Amazon can drop you from the service for hurting their image, something that you will obviously want to avoid at all costs.

Consider each purchase carefully: The best online retail arbitrage products are those that are heavily discounted, irrespective of the type of product in question. As a general rule, if you find anything, literally anything that is marked down 75 percent from its original price, then you can likely find a way to sell it for a profit online; whether it is worth it is another question. Another great choice are items that you can purchase in bulk cheaply now, before waiting for natural scarcity to set in six months or so down the line when your investment will pay off in spades.

A great example of this are toys you can purchase from a dollar store that are based on properties that are never going to go out of style such as Disney properties like Princesses, Star Wars or Marvel superheroes. Many of these products are only ever sold at dollar stores which means that after the initial stock dries up there will be thousands of parents out there looking for character specific merchandise that their child has not consumed yet. If you aren't interested in waiting, you can instead group a number of themed items together, knock a fraction of the total profit off and sell the total as a true bargain.

For example, if you purchase five Disney Princess puzzles for a total of $5, knowing that each typically sells for $5 on Amazon, then you can sell all five for $20, still have the group seen as the value, and even make more than a 50 percent profit on the transaction. If you pursue this course of action, you are going to generate a unique UPC code for the group of products, though you can use the same UPC code for multiple groups if applicable.

Don't forget about social media: The most essential social media for any company or brand to have is Facebook. Pretty much everybody uses Facebook, and having an active Facebook page is absolutely essential. Do whatever you can in order to build your Facebook fan base. Your posts aren't always going to get a ton of traction, but any traction and any traffic matters... plus, if you make a really good post, you're going to see a lot of traffic come from it naturally. That's just how it works with social media.

You're also going to want to consider getting Twitter and Instagram. These aren't quite as popular as Facebook and are more geared towards people in the 16 to 30 crowd, so if your niche aims at people who are older, then you may not have as much success on these. However, having a popular following on these networks can make a lot of difference for you as a company if you follow through with it appropriately and make a lot of posts.

Finally, you're going to want to set up a Snapchat. Snapchat is potentially one of the best marketing platforms because unlike other forms of social media, where only a portion of your followers can see your content without specifically going to your page, a story on Snapchat is visible to all of your followers. If you have a particularly visually appealing niche, Snapchat can be a great way to show people what you're up to and what's up next on your blog. This extra traffic and these return users will, in turn, lead to a big return on your affiliate marketing products.

CONCLUSION

Having reached the end, I can only be satisfied with the journey we have made together. I hope you are too.

And that's it for this book on how to make money with amazon fba. Remember that despite everything, this is a business that, if taken seriously, can lead you to sell for tens of thousands of euros.

You just have to overcome the initial difficulties and acquire a minimum of experience, progressively optimizing all processes.

Good work and good success!